Donald Trump's Top 10 Rules for Su

Ross Cameron

2nd Edition

Table of Contents

Introduction: Making the Man

Donald Trump was born in 1946 to Fred and Mary Trump in Queens, New York. His father started to build garages at age 16 and decided to go into real estate construction in his early twenties. Later, this company would be named Trump Organization LLC. As a boy, Trump was sent to the New York Military Academy. From there, he earned his Bachelor of Science degree in Economics from the University of Pennsylvania. Soon after, Trump joined his father's business and after some successful deals moved to Manhattan to establish his own career as an entrepreneur and business mogul. In 1980, he opened the Grand Hyatt and is now a very famous, and controversial, business figure. He is currently listed on the Forbes list of richest people, and has maintained himself as successful brand. In 1987, he wrote the book *The Art of the Deal*, which he claims is his second favorite book - the first being the Bible. He is a successful entrepreneur who has spent his adult life creating businesses, hotels, television shows, and is now in the running for President of the United States.

Now, Trump is running in the Presidential candidacy. No one knows if Trump will successfully become President, or what his Presidency would look like, but as a businessman, he has learned some great lessons that have helped him to gain the confidence to enter the campaign as a potential and real candidate. Though his party, the Republicans, are uncertain about his campaign and his stance, Trump has shown his popularity by being a frontrunner in the polls since he announced his involvement. He uses the lessons that he has learned as a developer and applied them to his political campaign. He uses the spectacle and bluntness in his everyday deals and his campaign speeches. In fact, it might be these lessons that have helped him to become a front running candidate so early in this election. Much of the public tend to view Trump's stance as a reflection of how he has successfully taken over the business world. In looking at Trump's tips to the public, it is easier to understand his own opinions, views, and how he has worked his way to become a top businessman and one of the richest men in America. His brand as a politician has come from all the years that he has built a brand out of his name and his business ventures.

Regardless of whether you agree with Trump as a businessman - or his platform as a potential President - it is important to appreciate the brand that he has built around his name and the legacy that is connected to this. He is a controversial figure, but that does not mean that his sentiments and beliefs need to be dismissed immediately. Trump's advice provides a well-rounded idea of how he feels people can be more successful. Rather, it means that he has used his experience to grow into a position, using his tactics, where he can generate opinions, glee, and outrage. Trump has built his empire through lessons that he has learned in his life, and he has presented ten of them to the public so that any entrepreneur can grow and hopefully build another empire of their own. Though his lessons are generally geared towards success in business, they also transition into how to lead happier, stronger lives.

Chapter 1: Is Money Important?

Trump's first lesson for the public is "don't do it for the money," or, for clarification, do not just do business for the money. Trump states that, "I don't do it for the money. I have got enough, much more than I will ever need. I do it to do it. Deals are my art form. Other people paint beautifully on canvas or write wonderful poetry. I like making deals, preferably big deals. That's how I get my kicks." In this quote, Trump compares business to art. This is important because in his 1987 book, *The Art of the Deal,* it exemplifies not just how Trump makes his deals but also how he views them. This helps to show why he doesn't necessarily need money -- especially since he claims to now have so much. Just as some artists do not paint for money, Trump does not do the business deals for money -- certainly not now anyhow.

Though Trump quite obviously shows an appreciation for money—as any true businessman does—he explains that money should not be the only reason to do business, or anything in life for that matter. He explicitly states, "I believe in spending what you have to. But I also believe in not spending more than you should." It is important to remember that though money is important, it is even more important to enjoy what you do—even if it means that you make a little bit less. Trump once stated, "the worst thing you can possibly do in a deal is seem desperate to make it. That makes the other guy smell blood and then you're dead. The best thing you can do is deal from strength." This quote really aligns with this ideology because if you are desperate for money, you become far more desperate to make the deal. Yet, if you are not making the deal for money, you lose the sense of urgency that might deter the other party from settling with you.

The importance of doing what you love is a recurring theme for Trump, who himself explains that though money is what keeps you in the game, it cannot be the sole driving force. You need to be able to focus on other aspects of what success means. For example, your integrity, your character, your ethics, your legacy, your family, are all ideas of what success can mean, and none of these aspects can be found commercially. In fact, most of these characteristics are not even tangible. Though money can get a lot of tangible items in this world, especially in today's society, it cannot buy everything. To prove this, Trump once said, "if it can't be fun, what's the point? Life is very fragile, and success doesn't change that. If anything, success makes it more fragile. Anything can change, without warning…" and if you rely too much on money to make those changes, you could lose a lot. Rather, rely on the experience and the intangible results, much like the ones listed above. Clearly, Trump has not been in a position where he has been short on money, yet, it does remain seen that when you enjoy what you do, it will be a far better experience than if you simply do it for money.

The most important thing to remember is that even though money may make it easier to be happy, it will not be the only thing that generates happiness. As shown above, Trump states, "if you can't be happy, what's the point?" This transcends more boundaries than a business perspective, and can easily become a mantra for every aspect of life. Trump has made it clear that if you find your passion, if you love what you do, that is far more important than making money.

The environment and people that you surround yourself with is what makes you happy, and it is crucial to "value loyalty above everything else." Trump expressly stated that he does things because he enjoys them, even if he might lose money or might not make any money. Rather, these tasks, which he does not specify, fulfill him in other ways and lead to him being a happier, better businessman. At the end of the day, money can only add so much to a person's life before they need to find something else.

Chapter 2: The Importance of Persistence

Secondly, Trump states to "never give up." This ties in with his belief that you should never take no for an answer. It is important to keep going, even when times seem difficult. He once stated, "I don't spend a lot of time worrying about what I should have done differently, or what's going to happen next. What do my deals add up to? I'm not sure, except that I have had a very good time making them." This lesson connects with the first one since there are real parallels that can be drawn between never giving up and not doing it for the money. As well, his quote shows that part of his success lies in not obsessing over his failed business deals, but rather embracing the opportunity for the next one and striving to reach it through hard work and determination.

There are going to be times in your life where it may not seem worth it to keep going, or you feel as though you are going to fail, or you are not making enough to continue on. Well, do not stop; rather "much as it pays to emphasize the positive, there are times when the only choice is confrontation" and it takes a lot of hard work to get to the point where you can both acknowledge and accept this reality. It is important to learn from your mistakes, as that is part of growing, but do not let these mistakes bring you down. For, as he says, "the world does not owe you anything. Everything needs to be deserved." Business is very cutthroat, and only the ruthless hard workers succeed. If you give up, you will be alienated by people who could help you.

If you are passionate about your goals, your interests, your dreams, keep going; even if all you get is experience. He, in fact, entitled one of his books, *Never Give Up.* It is important also to stay open to new information and new ideas, for "if you know your stuff... you will command instant respect." You never know where that experience will take you. He mentions that people who are on top are not generally the ones who got good grades easily in school. It is so easy to give up, to tear yourself down and focus on only the negative, but yet, it is far more fulfilling to continue working and believing that one day, it will get easier. Failure helps to build character, and will make it that much better when you succeed. The people who have persisted, even after failing, have been that much more grateful when they finally have worked their way to the top, because they remember their struggles and remember how much work it took to get there. To summarize, Trump once said, "Finding your purpose may be a lifelong pursuit or you may have discovered it when you were 5 years old. There's no absolute timeline for anyone. That's a good reason never to give up, to keep on discovering things every day." This sentiment seems to really cement why he does not give up, and why it is important not to give up. You learn more about yourself and about the world every single day that you continue on.

It is the people who failed and failed continuously, but yet, still managed to work their way to the top. Just like everyone else, Trump has had self-doubt, and "probably more than people would think. I understand how life can go. Things can happen." Yet, even with his self-doubt, he has refused to give up and has persisted in becoming one of the most recognizable brands in the world, certainly in the last 30 years. You will change as a person while this occurs, but yet, it is important to keep on course. If you don't give up, one day, you will reach a point where money does not have to matter at all. Before you get there though, you need to make sure that you truly believe in what you are doing and never stop. Further on, Trump will give further information on believing in yourself, but the important thing at this moment is to know the importance of continuing on, even when times are difficult. You will become a far better, and smarter, business person because of it.

Furthermore, never giving up does not simply translate to the business deals but also to the people who are behind the big businesses. Trump shows that "I'm very good to people who are good to me. But when people treat me badly or try to take advantage of me, my general attitude has been to fight back very hard." People are going to try to cut you down, especially when you gain more traction and success. You must fight back, and must not stop fighting "even if it means alienating some people along the way - things usually work out for the best." You must find out who will help assist you in success and who will not. You are only as successful as the people you surround yourself with, and if you stick with hard workers who did not give up in the face of adversity, you will be more successful and will be far less likely to give up. The important point is to not give up.

Chapter 3: It's All in the Details

Thirdly, details are crucial to success. They are an important aspect to establishing a business; for, it is the details that show the different calibre's between companies. Details are the framework to a solid business plan. Yet, Trump states that "the greatest of consulting firms charge you $100,000 for a lengthy study and in the end it has no conclusion and takes so long to complete that if the deal you were considering was a good one, it will be long gone," and so he points out that the details come from his own brain. He is the most invested in the deal -- it is his money and brand on the line -- and so, much like in his presidential campaign, he observes details from his own mind.

You may have an amazing overall plan, such as consulting firms, but if you do not even assess the tiniest reason why one aspect would not work, or something could go wrong, your whole plan could very quickly unravel. He once said, "Sometimes by losing a battle you find a new way to win the war." The attention is in the details, and if you focus on the details, the whole plan will come together far more soundly as a whole. Trump says that "I don't hire a lot of number-crunchers, and I don't trust fancy marketing surveys. I do my own surveys and draw my own conclusions. When I am in another city and I take a cab, I'll always make a point to ask the cabdriver questions. I ask and I ask and I ask, until I begin to get a gut feeling." The gut feeling and doing the surveys himself allows him the control to fully analyze all of the details so that he only holds himself accountable. He does not have anyone else to blame if a deal goes bad, and only himself to congratulate when a deal goes through and the details are perfected. You will also have far more control over any situation that might arise, and you can deal with the problem immediately.

If you do not begin by looking at details, they will "come back to haunt you later." He further explains that both business and life are made better when you ensure that you look at the details of any task. He explains, "My style of deal-making is simple. I aim very high, and then I just keep pushing and pushing and pushing to get what I'm after." He would not be able to push on his high goals if he did not consider every little obstacle and perfection in his dreams and goals.This lesson really transcends proper business etiquette and turns into advice on how a person should live their life. At the end of the day, Trump explains, if a person neglects the details in their life, relationships, business ventures, or school, that's where they can lose. In life, it is easy to get so caught up in your major goals that you miss the smaller tasks and accomplishments. This will affect how your big goals are achieved and what you learn from your experiences. Simply put, when it comes to work and life, you cannot ignore the details.

Chapter 4: Focus, Focus, Focus

In his next lesson, Trump explains that focus is paramount. You cannot lose focus; especially when you are under pressure. This lesson relates to the idea that if you truly want something bad enough, you will learn to stay focused - even when it is difficult. He explains, "one of the keys to thinking big is total focus. I think of it almost as a controlled neurosis, a quality I've noticed in many highly successful entrepreneurs. They're obsessive, driven and almost maniacal, but it's all channeled into their work." People can go near madness when completely focused, but, at the end of the day, it pays off. He further says, "I don't say this trait leads to happier life, or a better life, but it's great when it comes to getting what you want." Clearly, you need more traits than focus, but when you fixate on discovering the solution to a problem, you are far more likely to find it than if you just dilly dally and work on the problem whenever it tickles your fancy. You need to focus on the problem, the solution, the environment and the obstacles.

When describing this tip, Trump tells a story of a time when he diverted his attention from his business aspirations and instead spent all of his time and money with women, athletes, and celebrities. This lifestyle, he explains, was fantastic while the economy was good, but once it crashed, his company crashed with it. This happened because he was too focused on having a good time, rather than ensuring that his company was secure regardless of the economical situation. He once said, "to me it's very simple: if you're going to be thinking anyway, you might as well think big. Most people think small, because they're afraid of success, afraid of making decisions, afraid of *winning*."

It is through focus, composure, persistence, and attention to details -- all of the points already mentioned above -- that you become better able to win big and think big. Dreams become far more attainable through focus. Further, by keeping yourself focused, you are better able to handle the level of pressure that is required to excel as an entrepreneur. Focus is what drives you to keep your eye on the prize, and influences how you make all of your business decisions. Without that focus and determination, you are far more likely to become side-tracked, and becoming the number one-person industry becomes that much more difficult. Your lack of focus becomes a hurdle that you are putting in front of yourself.

Chapter 5: The People You Surround Yourself With

You are only as good as the people that you work with, and if you "set high standards for people... expect they will fulfill them." In many cases, as the boss, you need to hire people that you know will be a good decision for the face of your company, and will help to further your company through becoming part of the culture. Otherwise, as stated above, you may have to "*alienate*" some people along the way -- things usually work out for the best." Trump explains that, in his mind, the worst employees are what he calls the "good employees." He goes on to say that if you have bad employees, it is okay, because you can very quickly fire them. These employees simply drag you down, and it is an extremely easy decision. Trump once said, "In my life, there are two things I've found I'm very good at: overcoming obstacles and motivating good people to do their best work." These are two things that he needs both in business and politics, and so to be able to hire strong support, and know what you are looking for is vital.

Comparatively, great employees are insanely easy to keep since they help build your company and its culture. They are the people who maintain focus and attention to both the big picture and the miniscule details. They believe in the company, and its goals, with fervor and will work non-stop to ensure that the company will succeed. These employees are wonderful because they will do their job, and do it well. Even so, Trump says that it is ideal to hire great employees, but do not simply trust them.

The good employees are the ones to be wary and hesitant about. He explains that this is because good employees are stagnant. They do their job well enough that an employer cannot justify firing them; yet, they do not do well enough to help the company. They slide through their day, doing just enough work to stay on with the company. These are the employees that do not help the company to get ahead. These good employees strike the perfect balance between being a great and a bad employee. As Trump says, "only hire people with positive attitudes and get rid of the bad apples fast."

It is important to hone your skills on who you will be able to work well with, and build an empire with, and who will hold you and your company back. There will always be people who do the bare minimum to scrape by and stay completely mediocre, the goal is to minimize those employees so that your company can grow into a huge enterprise with strong leaders who will positively impact the company culture and experience. The important thing is to filter through the bad, and the good, employees to find the ones that shine.

Chapter 6: Hard Work = More Luck

In his next tip to success, Trump quotes a famous athlete who once said "I find that the harder I work, the luckier I get." Though Thomas Jefferson was the first to say this, the fact that an athlete and then Trump later quotes it, shows the universality of this statement. This phrase is one that has been uttered by many famous people. Essentially, it means that if you use the tools already described - staying focused, never giving up, looking at the details - you will be a harder worker. Eventually, after years of working hard and being dedicated, you will hopefully catch a break; and then, another break; followed by yet another. Though luck is definitely an intangible aspect that helps with success, it is not something that can be controlled.

You gain experience and knowledge when you work hard, and this leads to naturally better informed decision making, which, in turn leads to luckier odds at gaining a property or investing in a trade. Though, Trump also says, "del-making is an ability you're born with. It's in the genes. It's not about being brilliant. It does take a certain intelligence, but mostly it's about instincts. You can take the smartest kid... The one who gets straight A's and has a 170 IQ, and if he doesn't have the instincts, he'll never be a successful entrepreneur." If you have those instincts, and the knowledge that comes from years of experience, you will become far luckier in all of your deals.

Luck is based on the foundation of knowledge; in turn, knowledge comes from years of hard work. It is a strange connection, that two intangible feats equal to one tangible aspect, but it is important to know as you continue to work. Many people look at successful businesspeople, athletes, celebrities, and think about how lucky they are for their lifestyles, their careers, their possessions; yet, what the public does not see, and often forgets about, is how hard the person had to work to get there.

If you have big dreams, there is nothing wrong with that, but in order to achieve those dreams, so that you may one day attain the lifestyle that you desire, you need to push yourself - even when it seems hard or impossible. It matters that even if you wake up one morning and just want to stay in bed, because it's gloomy or you're tired, you still must get up and work towards your end goal. It is through this hard work that you will gain luck and experience. Unfortunately, dreams do not happen unless you identify how you can accomplish them and set goals for yourself to work towards. Even if your dream is not to become an athlete, or a business tycoon, the same rules still apply. It does not matter the size of your dreams, or aspirations, as long as you work hard enough, it will become more attainable and easier.

Trump once used this anecdote, "people think I'm a gambler. I've never gambled in my life. To me, a gambler is someone who plays slot machines. I prefer to own slot machines. I happen to be very conservative in business. I always go into the deal anticipating the worst. If you can live with the worst, the good will take care of itself." This anecdote works for a number of reasons. Firstly, gambling and luck are deeply connected and you cannot bring up one without associating the other to it. Trump secures the famous quote when he says this, as he defines gambling to fit into his world and to his idea of what gambling is. Through the lines, this quote explains that he bases his business on knowledge and experience -- not luck. He won't make a gamble because there is too much chance. His luck is not based on odds; instead, it is based on his ability to make a good business deal because he is equipped with the knowledge and ability to do so. His luck in life has come from his ability to stay away from gambling.

Chapter 7: Focus on your Feelings

Though working hard is a huge aspect of reaching your goals, there is one part of yourself that cannot be ignored for anything: your instincts. Trump once said, "you can have the most wonderful product in the world, but if people don't know about it, it's not going to be worth much. You need to generate interest and create excitement," and much of deciding who your target market is, or which outlet you will use to advertise this product, come from pure instinct. Of course, you can use consultants and marketing teams, but it is your gut feeling that tells you where to use them and how. As well, Trump once wrote, "Part of being a winner is knowing when enough is enough. Sometimes you have to give up the fight and walk away, and move on to something that's more productive." This is why he will continuously ask a cab driver questions until he begins to get a gut feeling.

One way in which Trump has been able to foster his gut feeling is through how he works. To explain, he says "many people are surprised by the way I work. I don't carry a briefcase. I try not to schedule too many meetings. I leave my door open. You can't be too imaginative or entrepreneurial if you've got too much structure. I prefer to come to work each day and just see what develops. There is no typical week in my life." He does not generate a complete schedule for the day, and this leaves room for him to be creative, and to let his instincts continue to tweak and grow. Furthermore, he says, "I usually arrive at my office by nine, and I get on the phone. There's rarely a day with fewer than fifty calls, and often it runs to over a hundred. In between, I have at least a dozen meetings, but the majority occur on the spur of the moment, and few of them last longer than fifteen minutes." This leaves him time to consider everything that has been said, and planned, through the day and allows Trump to make decisions based upon what his instincts tell him.

You need to foster your gut feeling and listen to it; otherwise, you may become more likely to make the wrong decisions. Trump allows himself a lot of time in the day to focus on his gut feeling and pay attention to what it says he should do. Your instincts are what help to guide you on what the best decision is for yourself. As you begin to gain experience, they affect you and your growth within the industry and within life. As such, it is important to pay attention to how your gut reacts to a person or a situation. Your hard work and experience directly impacts how your intuition reacts to a scenario. Trump once wrote, "sometimes your best investments are the ones you don't make," and that comes from an understanding of when to trust your gut and walk away - even if the deal sounds amazing.

For example, say that you are just attempting your first business venture, and you soon discover that you need funding. Perhaps, a bank would not be a viable option and so, you must find a private investor. This investor shows great enthusiasm for your endeavors, and promises to invest. Yet, when the time comes, he does not; instead, you find out that he does not actually have the money. Though this experience is not great for the moment, it does give you further insight for the future. You will learn not to be quite so trusting of a person's word without actually confirming that you can both meet the requirements of the arrangement. So, next time you are looking for an investor, your gut would say to check a person out fully so that you know that they will actually be able to follow through on the deal.

Your instincts will help you to succeed, they are an ally to hard work and focus. They will help you to continue going, as your instincts are an intrinsic part of you. Trump explains that there comes a point where, instead of listening to what your parents or friends say, you will instead focus on what your gut says and you will follow that instead. Trump understands that passion conquers fear, and the best way to know between the two -- history has shown that they sometimes get mixed up -- is to understand how your body reacts to them differently and similarly. Be in tune with how your body responds to positive and negative decisions, and let your feelings foster from there.

Chapter 8: You Are Important

Perhaps the most important lesson, and the one that all of these other pieces of advice have been working towards, is to believe in yourself. Trump exemplifies this when he says, "it's been said that I believe in the power of positive thinking. In fact, I believe in the power of negative thinking. If you plan for the worst -- if you can live with the worst -- the good will always take care of itself," and to be able to prepare for the worst, you have to be able to believe that you will successfully make it to the worst, even if it takes a few hurdles to do so. You need to constantly imagine yourself as victorious, and keep your eye on the prize. In his campaign, Trump once said to a reporter, "they want success. They wanted humility in the past. They wanted a nice person. But what they really want is someone who can win. We're going to have so many victories, you will be bored of winning." Only someone who truly believes in himself would be able to say this with so much enthusiasm and vigour.

It is a simple question: if you do not believe in yourself, then who else will? You are either your own biggest fan or your own worst enemy. It is up to you which one you want to be, and under which circumstances you want to believe in yourself. A reporter once wrote of Trump, "the ease with which Trump exhibits, and inhabits, his self-regard is not only central to his 'brand' but also highlights a kind of honesty about him." His self-regard comes from Trump's innate ability to believe in himself -- and what he can achieve -- through both good and bad times. What is the point in working hard and focusing all of your energy on achieving your goals - both in your career and personal life - if you do not even believe that you can achieve them?

You may have some huge obstacles to overcome, including public criticism, but as long as you believe in yourself and throw yourself into what you personally want to accomplish, the rest should not matter. As Trump once said, "the press is always hungry for a good story, and the more sensational the better. It's in the nature of the job. If you are a little different, or a little outrageous, or if you do things that are bold or controversial, the press is going to write about you." In order to be bold or controversial, you have to believe in your ability to become that important. You have to believe in yourself to get there, regardless of the method.

No one is going to build you up like yourself, for you live in your own head. In fact, Trump once wrote, "I try to learn from the past, but I plan for the future by focusing exclusively on the present. That's where the fun is." He uses his past for lessons to help his future, but he stays focused on his present which is how he has generated his success internationally. He uses his past and the potential of his future to build up his own present. It is up to you, and only you, to face your internal demons and overcome them. Sometimes it is extremely difficult to believe in yourself, and to understand that you are running your own show, but as soon as you realize it, and accept it, everything else becomes far more achievable and attainable. Trump further states that if you rely too heavily on other people, you will only be let down and disappointed.

Instead, you must work with the aspects of your life and career that you can control. You can only rely on yourself, as no one else will look after you the same way that you will. So, on a foundational level, believing in yourself is by far the most important element of Trump's success. This lesson ties very much into the notion of working hard for yourself and for your dreams.

It is that in order to be a winner, it is absolutely crucial that you think like a winner. You cannot think of yourself as a loser, or as someone who will not be able to succeed, that is how you intrinsically set yourself up for failure.

Chapter 9: Messy Desk, Creative Mind

In the following piece of advice, Trump uses his desk as an example of how he views himself as a winner. He makes a point of stating that anyone he knows that has been successful has had a messy desk. In fact, a messy desk has helped him to become a better businessperson and entrepreneur. In one article, a reporter describes walking into Trump's office where Trump "was standing behind a desk cluttered with papers, piles of recent magazines with him on the cover and a Trump bubblehead doll. You ever see guys with nothing on their desk? He said by way of explaining his messy one. 'They always fail. I don't know what it is. I've seen it for years.'" Though, initially, this may seem like a strange, and bold, statement, upon further reflection, it actually does make quite a bit of sense.

Trump may be onto something that is now being scientifically proven. Recent studies have shown that messiness can actually inspire creativity. In one study, "48 adults found that subjects in a messy environment came up with ideas '28% more creative' while creating a list of unconventional uses for ping pong balls, even though the two groups came up with the same number of ideas." Further, it is decided that a messy desk also helps to prioritize documents and items by importance, as, it is understood the most important documents would be on the top. As such, Trump's seemingly crazy theory actually makes quite a bit of sense. As well, since he prides himself on his ability to come up with a creative solution to a tough problem, this theory simply proves what he has been saying for over thirty years.

Also, though a desk may look messy to one person of the public, it may not be for someone else. For example, Trump describes his desk and states that he knows where everything is located on his desk - even if it might look like there is no order. In fact, there is an order and even though you or I may not know what the order is, the fact remains that Trump, and any other desk-owner, does. He explains that his desk is essentially an attachment of his body. Though, clearly, they are different entities, the desk is where he does all of his work. It is where Trump accomplishes all of the tasks that he sets forth to achieve.

His office, with his stacked magazines, trophies lined against a window, and memorabilia from sporting events, is where he brainstorms, makes business deals, signs contracts; it is a space where he works and leaves the outside world. It is okay that his desk is messy, for it means that he is actually doing work. Trump warns that when a desk is not messy, or, worse, there is nothing on it, that is when a person should be concerned. In that case, it means that they do not have enough stuff to do - not enough business - which translates to them being less successful. Trump credits his messy desk as an important part of his success and implores people to try and get a messy desk, for it means that they are too busy to keep it fully cleared. Just make sure not to lose any important documents.

Chapter 10: Nothing Without Love

Lastly, and this lesson connects with the earlier idea of not doing it for the money, is to ensure that you love what you do. When he is asked how he got to the point of the presidential campaign, Trump responds, "I have no idea. But I'm here now. And it's beautiful." He finds beauty in the propaganda, the media frenzy, the promoting of his brand, and the idea of America's future the way he perceives it should be. This quote shows that if you love something, you not only become far more likely to work harder in your position, but also to achieve far more. When you can merge passion with your career, you become far better equipped to accomplish great things, and to do so without having to sacrifice an ounce of happiness.

In his explanation of this, Trump uses the example of his friend's son. His friend's entire family was into heavy dealings with stocks, and it was assumed that his son would also join the family trade. However, his son loved to build things far more. He was pressured by his family to stay in stocks, and tried to excel at it, but after a year, he quit to pursue his own path. Though his father was very mad at him for leaving, the son became a far happier and better person because of his decision. If you love what you do, it solves a lot of problems about your career, your personal life, and your ongoing happiness. You work far harder if you are passionate about your job, and your heart is more into whatever decision you make - you are better invested in your position and your company.

If you believe in yourself, work hard, focus, and love what you do, you will be in a far better position to both build your career but also sustain it for a long period of time. This final lesson truly wraps up everything that he has said, so far, about how he has managed to build a multi-million-dollar brand. A journalist once wrote, "Trump might be the single most self-involved yet least introspective person I have ever met in my life, in or out of politics. I'm guessing he would say this is a good quality in a president. It spares him unglamorous details." He loves the pro's and con's of both his personality and his business. He manages to turn any criticism on himself into a compliment, and he loves to do that.

It is easy to see that he loves every single one of his endeavors. He genuinely enjoys everything that he does, and that is what has allowed him to never give up, and to only stray in focus for short periods, and to continuously work hard. He loves his messy desk, and he loves how he has become lucky, mainly as a product, and result, of his personal and professional successes. Trump has grown into his position because he loves playing the game, even though he says "there is never an easy way to success," and what's more, he equally loves winning the game.

Conclusion: In The End...

Though it is easy to say all of these inspiring, motivational lessons, it is far more difficult to execute them. So, does Trump truly abide by these rules? Well, he has made an internationally successful hotel chain, he has become a top business person, and his name is known worldwide. He would not have been half as successful if he did not at least partially believe in what he has said to the public. He is so successful that Peggy Noonan of the Wall Street Journal recently said, "if he loses 'he goes back to being Donald Trump, but even bigger." He believes that he can be bigger and this is what causes him to push. Every challenge is seen as something that he will be able to overcome. This is shown when he recently said, "the branding of our country is at an all-time low. Now, 'branding' might not be the most beautiful word to use, but the fact is the country has been labelled so badly." This shows that he views the Presidential candidacy to be just like a business deal. He preaches that, "you're generally better off sticking with what you know," and he knows how to stay focused on details and big pictures; believe in himself; love what he does; and, focus on more than money. This is why he has been so successful in both business and politics with the general public.

You cannot be successful unless you work hard and believe that you will be successful. You must "hang out with the big thinkers" and "speak out like a big thinker," and "always think of yourself as someone important." Even though Trump did inherit a small amount of wealth from his father, he could have easily spent that money, or saved it and done nothing, but instead he worked hard to build his family name and his company so that it all became a top brand in the world. He may have some cutthroat business tactics, but he used that as a way to creatively leverage a television show. In his campaign -- which actually lacks a lot of ideology -- he says, "empathy will be one of the strongest things about Trump. When I'm in that position, when we have horrible hurricanes, all kinds of horrible things happen, you've got to have empathy." As so, he shows not only that his gut feeling will help him to understand when to be empathetic; but also, he further confirms that he views his campaign as an extension of the Trump brand -- another sign of pushing for the big dreams, and his philosophy that "it is easier to do things on the large scale."

He may have a couple of failed business ventures, but this merely backs up his claim that you should never give up, and that failure is a part of building a corporate name, and excelling in the sector. He is willing to try anything, which is why, even without any prior political history, Trump is not only able to campaign, but is a frontrunner, for the Presidential candidacy in 2017. That stems for believing in what you are capable of doing, regardless of any challenges that might be presented along the way. He has money and he uses that as leverage to help show the public how successful he is. As he says, "leverage is something the other guy wants. Or better yet, needs. Or best of all, simply can't do without. Unfortunately, this isn't always the case, which is why leverage often requires imagination and salesmanship." It is easy to see that Trump is using his concept of leverage in life, in work, and in politics - with varying degrees of success.

Trump has been able to maintain focus on exactly what he wants, and has made small goals along the way to obtain his wishes. The reason why he is able to spend time with models, athletes, celebrities and politicians is because of how hard he has worked to show that he is worthy of spending time with them; or, rather, they are worthy of spending time with him. He has "been open to new information and new ideas," focused on details, and that is how, even with some failed business ventures that might have essentially killed a business, he is able to stay afloat and booming. He has kept his name relevant through all of these beliefs and through following his mantras.

Regardless of how people think of him as a person, there has to be something said about his resilience and his ability to keep on advancing, even if the rest of the world is seemingly against him. This is because he looks to his internal self and the instincts that he has built up through years of experience as a pioneer and entrepreneur. His history shows that he practices what he preaches, even if it doesn't necessarily work out for him all of the time.

In his lessons, Trump has shown some ongoing themes. Mainly, all of his words of advice have to do with internal factors. Not a single one of his lessons have to do with the outside world, except to "never forgive a crook," but rather what you can do to control your personal growth and the growth of your company. His advice continuously requires you to look inside yourself to discover what makes you happiest and how you can find that happiness, such as "what you dream is what you will do," and "be willing to face new challenges," and, most importantly, "avoid negative thinking."

In every example, he makes a point of not mentioning any outside factors, because you cannot control the world around you, all that you can control is how you react to your environment. Secondly, a lot of his key concepts and advice stems around pushing yourself mentally and physically. It takes a lot of work to build a working business, but if you are able to push yourself and keep pushing, you will be far more likely to succeed than those who simply give up because it is too hard. Trump did not create a brand like his simply on a whim; he worked hard to specialize in business, to use leverage and salesmanship, to grow the confidence that borders on arrogance, to become the megastar that he is today. He draws in crowds because he has worked so hard to learn how. He has had to sell both himself and his product in order to make the brand as successful as it is today.

One thing that Trump is very blunt about is the amount of work that it takes to maintain a sustainable business, and that you need to choose the right team to help you once you have established your starting point. His other main theme is the theme of confidence. One trait that Trump continues to maintain, regardless of any scandal, is confidence that he will get the job done. Trump truly is his own biggest fan, and not in a negative way. He believes that he is the best person to build hotels, or run reality TV shows (such as his hit show, The Apprentice), or run a country; even if he does fail, he simply tries again until he succeeds. That is because of his confidence and his total belief in himself. Trump's experiences have only helped foster his self-identification as a collected man who has the ability to own the world if he wishes. He is an example of how his own beliefs can apply to the real world - even his messy desk.

To summarize, though Trump's internal tactics may not equip you with all of the tools that you need to be as successful as he is, they may lead to some food for thought. His tools and tips may be exactly what you, as a blooming entrepreneur, need to hear in order to feel inspired to establish your own name in the business world. It is re-assuring to know that he too has failed, but it is only through persistence and determination that he has managed to continuously re-build himself. Clearly, other things, such as knowledge of the business world, terminology, and ethical practices are important to learn.

The technical aspects, however, will build upon the foundation that your intrinsic beliefs have set. Remember, it is important to think that you will succeed. You are far more likely to do so if you think that you can. Alternatively, if you try, and find that you do not love being an entrepreneur, it is perfectly acceptable to try something else until you have found what truly makes your heart and soul happy. At the end of the day, as long as you can say that you tried and that you never gave up, that is what matters, and that is what Trump is trying to say when he states all ten of those lessons. That is why they are so deeply imbedded with what your mind thinks, and your own feelings, and determination.

Trump believes that he can do anything that he sets out to do, and that belief is what has gotten him to the point where he is in his life. It is that unwavering devotion to yourself, and that mentality, that will lead to success moving forward in your career. If you don't focus on believing in yourself, no one else will believe in you, and you will have to face a lot more challenges than if you simply admit to yourself that your goals are attainable. If you do not believe in yourself, or take any risks, in any aspect in life, you will only hold yourself back. You can hold yourself back more than anyone else can, and Trump does not allow himself to be held back by anyone or anything, including himself. To summarize, Trump wrote in his 1987 book, "The final key to the way I promote is bravado. I play to people's fantasies. People may not always think big themselves, but they can still get very excited by those who do. That's why a little hyperbole never hurts." Perhaps, that is the actual secret to his success.